How to survive
PARENTHOOD

Clive Whichelow & Mike Haskins

Illustrations by Kate Rochester

summersdale

HOW TO SURVIVE PARENTHOOD

Summersdale Publishers Ltd
46 West Street
Chichester
West Sussex
PO19 1RP
UK

www.summersdale.com

Printed and bound in China

ISBN: 978-1-84953-137-5

Substantial discounts on bulk quantities of Summersdale books are available to corporations, professional associations and other organisations. For details contact Summersdale Publishers by telephone: +44 (0) 1243 771107, fax: +44 (0) 1243 786300 or email: nicky@summersdale.com.

To My Super Mummy

On Your Very First Birthday With Me

From "CHEEKY" LEO. T.

X X X
X X
X

Other titles in this series:

How to Survive Marriage
How to Survive Retirement
How to Survive University

INTRODUCTION

Oh, it's going to take some getting used to, this parenthood lark, isn't it? The crying, the waking up in the middle of the night, the tantrums — and once the baby starts all that as well it'll be even worse.

But no, all jesting aside, this is the start of the most amazing experience of your life. Your friends will have told you all the horror stories about the terrible twos, the frantic threes, the flippin' fours, and the fearsome fives, but that's only part of it. You'll have the scary sixes, the surly sevens, the evil eights and all the rest as well.

And then there's the good stuff: baby's first smile (ah!), baby's first tooth (ouch!), and baby's first birthday. Before you know it you'll have thousands of photographs of baby's first everything — well, maybe not quite *everything*... And you'll say a silent thank you to the inventor of the digital camera. Where *would* you have stored them all? Happy parenting!

THINK POSITIVELY

For the first couple of years your child
will not answer back — make the
most of it!

You will soon be an expert in something,
like nappy changing with one hand on a
windswept beach in Bognor!

At last you have an excuse to play on the see-saw and the swings at the park again

SELF-HELP BOOKS YOU MIGHT WANT TO READ

Perfect Parents: A Guide to Spotting Their Flaws

An Introduction to Hypnosis to Get Small Children and Teenagers to Behave

Is Your Baby Having a Bawl? (And How to Sleep Through It)

Homework: A Parents' Guide to Getting It Right

EMBRACE PARENTHOOD
WITH A GOOD DOSE
OF IRONY

Year after year keep on buying your kids
toys that are obviously really for you
to play with, such as a lawnmower or a
surround-sound home cinema system

New dads: get a pipe and tartan slippers;
new mums: a cashmere twin set, pearls
and a bob haircut

Carry on conversing with your child in
nonsensical baby talk, even when they're
doing their A levels

TYPES OF PARENTING STYLE TO TRY

The angry brigade — who can be seen and heard having a swearathon with their children in a packed supermarket aisle

The busy, busy bees — who have drawn up a timetable for their children showing organised activities for every hour of every day for the next 18 years

Dippy hippy — who gives them a glass of Chardonnay with their dinner from age six and lets them have a tattoo before they can spell it

GOOD AND BAD
ROLE MODELS FOR PARENTS

Good	Bad
Parents who teach their children what's right and what's wrong	Parents who regularly have police cordon tape round their house
Parents who won't let their children eat junk food	Parents who think the 'twizzler' is a part of a turkey's anatomy
Parents who help their children with their homework	Parents who do all their children's homework and get competitive with other parents who are doing the same
Parents who turn days out into an adventure	Parents who strap their kids to barrels and push them over waterfalls

IRRITATING THINGS OTHER PEOPLE WILL START SAYING TO YOU

'They don't come with an instruction manual, you know!'

'With a bit of luck they'll be off your hands by the time they're forty!'

'Do you know how much it costs to bring
up a child these days?'

'Don't worry. If you have any more kids,
they'll probably be different!'

THINGS IT'S BEST NOT TO CONTEMPLATE

The fact that from now on people will refer to you not by your name but as your child's mum or dad

The number of embarrassing details about you that your darling child is going to proudly pass on to friends and family

Having to give the sensible grown-up
response when your child asks you to buy
them a mini motorbike or a tiger cub

REALISTIC AND UNREALISTIC GOALS IN YOUR NEW LIFE

Realistic: Bringing up a happy, contented child

Unrealistic: Bringing up a Nobel Prize winner who also scores the winning goal in the World Cup

Realistic: Expecting your baby to eventually settle into a sleep pattern

Unrealistic: Expecting to get more than four hours' unbroken sleep a night for the first year

Realistic: Having a teenager with
good manners

Unrealistic: Having a teenager who invites
you to share their tent at Glastonbury

BASIC LESSONS
TO REMEMBER

Whatever one expert says about child-rearing you will find another expert who says exactly the opposite

Any advice you get about babies from your parents will be several decades out of date — on the other hand, you've survived haven't you?

When your child learns to say its first words, this will be a magical moment — they will then go on to say them a thousand times until they have driven you insane

Any idiot can have a baby, but it takes a true idiot to have a whole family by accident!

Babies have no concept of time — it may be the middle of the night to you, but to them it's snack o'clock

TRICKS TO MAKE OTHERS THINK YOU KNOW WHAT YOU'RE DOING

Pretend your child has an obscure syndrome that accounts for every type of behaviour they exhibit, however extreme

Nod sagely every time your child does something odd and mutter 'ah yes...'

Consult your watch when giving your child a sweetie so others will think you are rationing their intake

If your child has a screaming fit, join in and pretend it's a form of ethnic singing

Tell people your child's terrible behaviour
is all part of a scientific study

HARD TRUTHS

Your child will still be your child when they're 60 and you'll have to be careful not to keep giving advice — although by that time you'll probably have started giving advice to the grandchildren

You can't choose your children — it's a lucky dip with the occasional booby prize

You will learn from your mistakes —
unfortunately your children will have to
live with them, such as calling them Daisy
Petal Foo Foo Banana

Your children have a natural desire to
challenge authority — and unfortunately,
as far as they're concerned, you are
that authority

SCIENTIFIC FACTS
ABOUT PARENTHOOD

If women eat fish during pregnancy it can
improve the baby's communication skills
(which probably explains why sea lions
are such great conversationalists)

Men are almost twice as fast as women
at changing nappies (this may be because
they are hurrying to get to the pub)

A newborn baby's head accounts for a
quarter of its weight (this soon changes
when it discovers fast food)

READY RESPONSES FOR COMMENTS AT THE SCHOOL GATE

'My children are in bed by six every night!'
'After a day with you that must be a welcome relief for them!'

'I don't let mine have anything containing E numbers.'
'Oh! So they're naturally hyperactive, then?'

'My youngest was walking by
six months!'
'That's because he wanted to get away
from you as soon as possible!'

'I think my child might be
another Einstein.'
'Yes, his hair does look a bit unkempt,
doesn't it?'

'My child comes first in everything
at school.'
'Well she was certainly the first to have
head lice.'

'I think he gets his brains from his father.'
'Yes, heredity can be so unfair, can't it?'

STARTLING STATS AND CAUTIONARY TALES

Newborn babies double in height within a year. If this keeps happening, consult a doctor — by the time your child is ten they will be 31 miles tall!

The cost of bringing up a child is estimated to be between £193,000 and £200,000. So before getting pregnant, try shopping around to get the best deal

Children usually start using a potty at the age of two. It is more difficult toilet training boys because they have to wee while standing up and aim into the bowl. Many grown men still haven't mastered this ability

When a child is five they probably need around 11 hours' sleep a night. By the time they reach 13, they will need nine a night. By the time they are students, they will need very little sleep at night but quite a lot during the day

There may be around 130 million children born in the world each year. By a happy coincidence, however, yours will be the most special and gifted of all of them

THINGS TO LOOK FORWARD
TO WHEN THEY
FLY THE NEST

Not having to listen to ear-splitting
'music' and worry about whether they've
crashed your car

The day your phone bill is only two pages
and not the length of a *Harry Potter* book

Buying pristine white furniture and dry-
clean-only clothes

THINGS YOU'LL FIND YOURSELF WORRYING ABOUT

UNIMPORTANT	IMPORTANT
Your baby is sucking its thumb and crying	Your partner is sucking their thumb and crying
Your child has an imaginary friend	Your friend has an imaginary child
Your child doesn't seem to be eating enough	Your child has just eaten the contents of the bathroom cabinet
Your child's head is a slightly odd shape	Your child's heads are slightly odd shapes

FIRST DAY DISASTERS
TO AVOID

Putting the nappy on the wrong end

Taking the baby off to the pub to celebrate and seeing if it fancies pie and chips on the way home

Giving your baby the most bizarre, ridiculous name you can think of

DOS AND DON'TS

Do use baby sign language with
your child

Don't end up with the only child to give
their nursery school teacher the finger

Do encourage your child to
be independent

Don't book them on an SAS-style survival
course before they begin primary school

Do teach your child to be strong and stand up for themselves with their friends

Don't encourage their friends to refer to your child either as 'The Godfather' or 'She Who Must Be Obeyed'

CHANGES THAT WILL HAPPEN TO YOUR APPEARANCE

You will have broken bits of toys poking out of every pocket

Your body will balloon due to sampling the kids' smiley potatoes, ice cream, jelly and assorted sweets

Your hair will look like it's styled by a small child — and for a very good reason

NEW FRIENDS YOU SHOULD TRY TO MAKE

Other people with kids who will understand when you fall asleep face first in your dinner

People of your own age and interests who just happen to be medically qualified and don't mind popping round at any time of the day or night

Someone who works in the buying
department of a large toy retailer

People with children who behave
noticeably worse than yours, so you don't
feel so bad about things

MOMENTS WHEN YOU MAY HAVE TO TRY AND CONTROL YOUR TEMPER

When your children first discover that
food makes a satisfying splat
when thrown

When you find a soggy rusk inserted in
the DVD player

When you discover someone has played
at cleaning your car with a Brillo pad

When your teenage children advertise their party on Facebook and the SAS has to be called out to disperse the crowds

When your four-year-old tuts and shows you how to use the computer properly

WHAT TO DO IF IT ALL GETS TOO MUCH

Remember, if you really need them to behave, small children are very easy to bribe!

Stand back, take a deep breath and count up to ten... or if necessary maybe keep counting until they're 21

Lock yourself in a quiet, dark room. If the kids haven't locked you in one already

HOW TO AVOID GETTING STUCK IN A RUT

Remember — for your kids, you are the perfect parent!

Resist the urge to blow raspberries on your child's tummy — especially once they've grown up

Manage, against all the odds, to keep calm

Just say 'whatever' when your kids smash
your favourite ornament

Go on an entire car journey without
pointing out sheep, horses or tractors
(easier as they get older) or reading every
road sign that you pass

Take them to a restaurant that doesn't
have a 'kidz menu'

ARGUMENTS YOU WILL FIND YOURSELF FALLING INTO WITH YOUR CHILDREN

'Father Christmas won't be coming!'

'You'll do it because I say so!'

'It's different for mummies and daddies!'

'We're not made of money, you know!'

'I don't care what time your friends
stay up till!'

IMPORTANT THINGS
TO REMEMBER

Your children like to wind you up like
they wind up their toys — it makes you
more entertaining

If they behaved well all the time, had
impeccable manners and common sense,
they wouldn't be children

However young you actually are, to your kids you're just this side of senility

To your children the word 'parent' has the same meaning as 'traffic warden' or 'tax inspector' does to you

Your kids can't be that weird — they're
miniature versions of you

DO SOMETHING PARENTS AREN'T SUPPOSED TO DO

Well, you could try getting a decent
night's sleep for a start

Stop thinking you always have to be the
authority figure and have fun being
a big kid

Get them to push you on the swings
for a change

Teach them to play online poker

Join in making a huge mess (your partner or your own parents will probably clear it up for you!)

FANTASIES YOU MAY START HAVING

It's all been a dream

The hospital will call to say there's been a mix-up and you were given the wrong baby!

Nanny McPhee will come and sort
everything out

You are a world-renowned child-rearing
expert who has been given a particularly
difficult case study

DON'T TRY TO LIVE UP TO AN IMPOSSIBLE IDEAL

Other children were not really talking, walking, reading Shakespeare, etc. quite as early as their parents may have told you

Parents as depicted in TV adverts only
look as happy, enthusiastic and clean as
they do because they are being paid to!

If the family next door seems perfect,
it's only because their house has better
soundproofing than yours

LITTLE WAYS TO LIFT YOUR SPIRITS

Begin finding the looks of horror on other parents' faces amusing

Look on your children's constant questions as a test of your general knowledge skills

Remember how much better your kids are
than some other people's

Repeat the words 'things will get better,
things will get better' until you start
to believe it

THE GOOD NEWS

However much they act up, your kids love
you really!

You are the most important people
in their lives (yes, even when they're
shouting 'I hate you!')

They grow up remarkably quickly (and once they do, you'll wish they were little again!)

www.summersdale.com